First published in the United States of
America by:

Twin Lights Publishers, Inc.
8 Hale Street
Rockport, Massachusetts 01966
Telephone: (978) 546-7398
http://www.twinlightspub.com

ISBN: 1-885435-73-8
ISBN: 978-1-885435-73-6

10 9 8 7 6 5 4 3 2 1

Up, Up, and Away *(opposite)*

It's a beautiful sight from ground level,
but from a balloon pilot's vantage
point, it's an exciting, competitive
event. Every July, the Ohio Challenge
Hot Air Balloon Festival attracts over
70,000 people.

(jacket front)

John A. Roebling Suspension Bridge

(jacket back)

Six bridges cross the Ohio River to link
Cincinnati with the cities of Newport
and Covington in northern Kentucky.

Editorial researched and written by:
Francesca and Duncan Yates
www.freelancewriters.com

Book design by:
SYP Design & Production, Inc.
www.sypdesign.com

Printed in China

Cincinnati was destined for crowning achievements from its very beginnings. Settled in 1788 on the northern bank of the Ohio River, the city is surrounded by seven, gentle hills that afford magnificent views in all directions. Its riverside location made it an accessible destination for newcomers from the east, a port of trade for growing commerce in the Northwest Territory, and a practical stopping point for those continuing on farther west.

By 1820, Cincinnati became America's first major "boom town." With the advent of steamboat navigation and the Miami and Erie Canals, it was the first western city to rival the early colonial cities of New England and the Mid Atlantic in size and wealth. In Mark Twain's era, the city docks were crowded with riverboats dropping off and picking up passengers and freight. Cincinnati soon became a major riverboat shipyard as well as the country's center for processing pork products. Referred to as "The Queen of the West" by a local newsman, poet Henry Wadsworth Longfellow embraced the phrase in a work about the new metropolis, quickly acquainting the rest of the country with its royal status.

Since its inception, the city has grown well beyond its original seven hills with over 300,000 residents in the city proper and nearly three million in the Greater Cincinnati area. Many major corporations are headquartered here, including Proctor and Gamble, which opened for business in 1837.

Cincinnati is now polishing up her diadem with a master plan that is revitalizing block after block of downtown with new museums, performance centers, athletic stadiums, beautiful parks, and residential neighborhoods. On the opposite side of the Ohio River, Cincinnati's northern Kentucky neighbors are following suit and stimulating their riverfronts with numerous entertainment and cultural attractions.

The crown of the "Queen of the West" shines in all of its glory through the expressive photography of native Cincinnatian, William Manning. Each colorful page captures Cincinnati's enduring majesty.

Cincinnati Museum Center

With its magnificent cascading fountain, Cincinnati Museum Center was once the Union Terminal, bustling with busy passenger trains. The hub of three museums, its updated façade incorporates a modernized beaux-arts classical style, bucking the neoclassical design trend.

Park Place at Lytle (*above*)

A distinctive, urban sculpture graces the entrance to the new, upscale Park Place at Lytle, a condominium renovation of an office building. An elegant lobby and uniformed doorman set the tone for downtown living with fabulous amenities, all within walking distance of the city's best attractions.

Historic Spires (*opposite*)

Completed in 1845, St. Peter in Chains Cathedral is one of the most striking examples of neo-classical Greek revival structures in the country. The cathedral has been the site of the ordination of many bishops as Catholicism moved westward, creating new dioceses. Its neighbor, City Hall, (*right*) is a remarkable, stone structure in the Romanesque style with rounded arches and a tower. Since its opening in 1893, City Hall has attracted a steady stream of admirers who come to see the exquisite, stained-glass windows throughout the building.

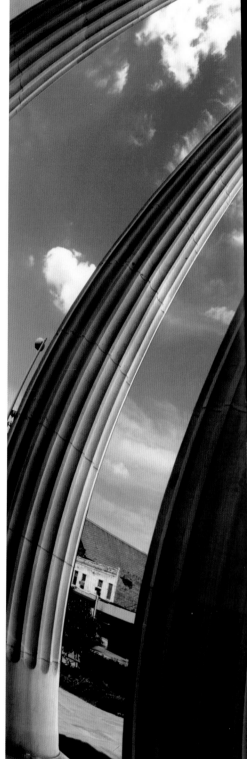

Bronze Icon

A bronze relief of Columbus' ship, *Santa Maria*, floats in a sea of columns of the Western and Southern Life Insurance Company building on East Fourth Street. The company aquired Columbus Mutual Life Insurance Company and their handsome company icon.

Plum Street Temple

A fisheye lens bends the columns of St. Peter in Chains Cathedral, and frames the Plum Street Temple. Built in 1866, the temple, and Cincinnati itself, quickly gained recognition as a national center of Judaism, thanks to legendary rabbi, Isaac Mayer Wise. Its prominence continues today as the region's largest Jewish congregation. The landmark temple is one of two remaining in the United States that were designed in the Byzantine-Moorish style, popular with German synagogues in the 19th century. The style recalls the influence of the Golden Age in Spain in Judaic history.

Flying Pigs at Sawyer Point Park (*above*)

The entrance to Cincinnati's scenic Bicentennial Commons at Sawyer Point Park is flanked with four steamboat stacks, each topped with a flying pig sculpture, in honor of Cincinnati's once-thriving hog processing and packing industry. Locals still affectionately refer to the city as "Porkopolis."

John A. Roebling Suspension Bridge (*opposite*)

Cincinnati's landmark suspension bridge over the Ohio River was designed by noted architectural engineer, John A. Roebling. Completed in 1866, the bridge introduced Roebling's ground-breaking engineering ideas which were also incorporated into his design for New York's Brooklyn Bridge.

Reflections of A Boom Town (*pages 12–13*)

Crowds of Greater Cincinnati residents celebrate each Labor Day along the banks of the Ohio, waiting for fireworks to be launched from a river barge alongside the Taylor Southgate bridge. While they wait, the city lights illuminate the skies and provide festive, colorful reflections on the river.

Reflections on Glass (opposite)

The Carew Tower is reflected in the glass and steel façade of the Fifth Third Bank Tower. Ground-breaking for Carew Tower occurred one month before the 1929 stock market crash. Construction continued, but plans for the façade's art-deco embellishments were abandoned after the third floor.

PNC Bank Building (top)

Located at Fourth and Vine, the PNC Bank building was the fifth-tallest building in America when erected in 1913. Home to the Union Central Life Insurance Company, it was referred to as the Central Trust Tower until it was acquired by PNC Bank in 2000.

Cincinnati's Tallest Skyscraper (bottom)

Upon its completion in 1931, the Carew Tower replaced the Central Trust Tower (now PNC Bank) as the city's tallest building. It is the city's most recognized landmark. The observation deck on the 50th floor offers panoramic views of the city and parts of Kentucky, Indiana, and Ohio.

People Bridge (top)

The Newport and Cincinnati railroad bridge opened in 1872, connecting Cincinnati and Kentucky. In 1904, it was refitted for auto traffic and renamed the Louisville and Nashville Bridge. Closed in 2001, it reopened as a pedestrians-only trestle in 2003, and includes a catwalk 140 feet above the river.

Purple People Bridge (bottom)

During redesign as a pedestrian walkway, a dozen focus groups were polled regarding the bridge's elements. The results ultimately defined the color selection and the evolution of its local nickname. The official name of the "Purple People Bridge" is the Newport South Bank Bridge.

The View from Kentucky *(above)*

The Ohio River is the watery boundary separating
Cincinnati from its northern Kentucky neighbors.
The gigantic Taylor-Southgate Bridge stretches
across the river, connecting the arts and culture of
Cincinnati and the wonderful cultural activities in
Newport, Kentucky.

Cincinnati from the River *(pages 18–19)*

Named for sponsor, Great American Insurance,
Great American Ball Park is home to the beloved
Cincinnati Reds National League baseball team. In
2003, the state-of-the-art facility replaced Cinergy
Field/Riverfront Stadium which the Reds had shared
with the NFL's Cincinnati Bengals since 1970.

Historic Towers of Cincinnati *(opposite)*

A clearer, more detailed view of the city's architectural history is seen from several stories above the street. On the left, the dark stone clock tower of the landmark City Hall (1893) rises in harmony with the bell tower of historic St. Paul's Church (1850), now the Verdin Bell and Clock Museum.

Musical Elegance *(top)*

Located in Over-the-Rhine, an historic German neighborhood, the magnificent Cincinnati Music Hall was built in 1878 in the High Victorian Gothic Revival style with Germanic touches. A world-class venue, it is the home of the Cincinnati Symphony, Cincinnati Opera, and the May Festival Chorus.

American Boom Town *(bottom)*

The massive, twin towers of Procter and Gamble's world headquarters fill the skyline behind the bell tower of the Verdin Bell and Clock Museum. As of 2006, P&G employs 100,000 people and is ranked 24th in size in the Fortune 100 roster of American companies.

Belle of Cincinnati (top)

A ride aboard the *Belle of Cincinnati* transports passengers back to the romance and adventure of riverboat life on the Ohio River during the 1800s. *Belle* is the grand dame of a Cincinnati-based fleet of steamboats that provide unforgettable sightseeing tours.

Riverboat Reunion (bottom and opposite)

Dozens of colorful paddle-wheelers and riverboats dock downtown after another day of celebration during Cincinnati's famous Tall Stacks Festival. The party began in 1988 when the city of Cincinnati invited riverboats from other cities on the Mississippi and Ohio rivers to help celebrate her bicentennial. One by one, the romantic steamboats converged on the Cincinnati waterfront, evoking sweet memories of the Mark Twain era. The festival stirred up so much excitement and pride among the riverfront communities that it soon became a regular event.

Lois & Richard Rosenthal Contemporary Arts Center

The stunning design of the new home to the Contemporary Arts Center was hailed by the *New York Times* as "the most important American building completed since the end of the Cold War." Inside, the center exhibits the works of bold, cutting-edge, artists. In 1940, the CAC became one of the first American institutions to show Picasso's *Guernica* (1937). Since then, Cincinnatians have been the first to view early works of artists such as Rauschenberg, Warhol, Jasper Johns, and Robert Morris.

Aronoff Center

The new Aronoff Center: DAAP at the University of Cincinnati almost doubles the space of the university's existing buildings and unifies the schools of Design, Art, and Architecture and Planning. Peter Eisenman created a building that challenges people to re-think their relationship with architecture.

One for All, and All for One

D'Artagnan, the narrator of Alexander Dumas' famous novel, *The Three Musketeers*, is the mascot of Xavier University's athletic teams. Xavier was founded in 1831 as the region's first Catholic institution of higher learning. Today, over 6,500 students attend this Jesuit school.

Vontz Center for Molecular Studies

The bulging walls of the Frank Gehry-designed Vontz Center at the University of Cincinnati Medical Center create a structure that is more sculpture than building. The Vontz Center is the research hub for new studies and discoveries in genetic and molecular mechanisms.

Historic Architecture *(top)*

The spires of the Music Hall rise in sharp contrast to the slow curve of the beaux-arts Cincinnati Museum Center at Union Station. The Music Hall continues to function as a grand performance space in the national historic district of Over-the-Rhine, a German-American neighborhood.

Flying Pig Marathon *(bottom)*

The marathon's course meanders through the streets of Cincinnati, continuing through Covington and Newport in Kentucky. Some of the city's flying-pig sculptures, located along the route, are an encouraging reminder to participants that anything is achievable.

Proctor and Gamble World Headquarters

A household name around the world, Proctor and Gamble was founded in Cincinnati in 1837, when candle maker William Proctor, and soap maker James Gamble went into business together. As the need for candles lessened, this consumer products giant began to focus more on soaps, and, during the 1880s, invented Ivory, the original "floating soap." During the early years of radio, Proctor and Gamble began sponsoring radio dramas which led to the coined term, "soap operas."

Sawyer Point

Along the shore of the Ohio River, just south of
downtown, is Sawyer Point—a mile-long park with
award-winning landscaping. Cincinnatians enjoy
the playground, tennis and volleyball courts, an
ice-skating rink, and outdoor concerts at the
acclaimed P&G Pavilion.

Skyline Frame *(above)*

The view of the downtown skyline, through the Beard Bridge, highlights several of the city's most well-known buildings—the PNC Tower to the left, the Atrium Towers, the Carew Tower behind the US Bank building, the Chemed Center, and the Center at 600 Vine to the far right.

Spanning the Ohio River *(pages 32–33)*

Six major bridges connect "Cincy" to northern Kentucky towns that are part of Cincinnati's greater metropolitan area. In the mid 1800s, when the city was the thriving shipbuilding and pork-processing capital of the West, the Ohio River was busy with steamboat traffic. In a single day, dozens of boats would drop off and pick up passengers and freight. For a fee of two dollars, an adventurer could buy a ticket to any town along 16,000 miles of inland waterway. At the height of the era, more than 11,000 paddle-wheelers navigated the waters of the Mississippi and Ohio rivers.

The Skater

Four figures at the base of the Tyler Davidson Fountain, located in Fountain Square, portray children taking pleasure in water-oriented activities. Traditionally, water flows from both hands of the robed woman atop the fountain. Lights drench the figures in winter when Cincinnatians gather to celebrate the "Lighting of the Fountain" ceremony. The city's central gathering place, Fountain Square has been revitalized with new facilities adjacent to the area's world-class hotels, shops and restaurants.

Tyler Davidson Fountain

Fountain Square, with its magnificent Tyler Davidson Fountain, is the heart of the city. The 34-foot-tall fountain was donated in 1871 by Cincinnatian, Henry Probasco, and named for his late brother-in-law. The elaborate sculpture celebrates the blessings of water, as it cascades down from the hands of its revered nine-foot focal point, *The Genius of Water*, by German, August von Kreling. Beneath her pedestal, figures by Ferdinand von Mueller depict the practical and joyful uses of water.

GARFIELD

President Garfield at Piatt Park *(opposite)*

Local sculptor Charles H. Niehaus created this imposing statue of Ohio native, James Garfield, twentieth president of the United States. The city's first public park, it is now the first "Wi-Fi" park; people with wireless cards in their laptop computers are able to log on to the Internet at no cost.

Eden Park *(above)*

Lined with flowering trees, a meandering path in Eden Park leads to an historic water tower. It was designed in the Romanesque Revival style and served the city until 1912. Eden Park is a lovely, spacious park and home to the renowned Cincinnati Art Museum and the Krohn Conservatory.

Ault Park

Ault Park is a favorite destination for Cincinnatians with its nature trails, picnic areas, and playgrounds. The park, surrounded by the beauty of formal, English gardens, is the site of the Summer Dance Series.

Ault Park Pavilion (top)

This stately pavilion commands the hilltop with a magnificent panoramic view of Ault Park's acclaimed gardens and beyond. Much to the delight of Cincinnatians, the 1930 pavilion has been fully restored to its former grandeur—the perfect crown for this stately treasure.

Tall Stacks Festival (bottom)

Young girls in 19th-century costume greet visitors at Cincinnati's famous Tall Stacks Festival, a celebration of the bygone steamboat era. Numerous public events reflect the city's pride in its history and culture.

Krohn Conservatory *(above)*

This spectacular atrium conservatory, located in the middle of Eden Park, allows visitors to experience the natural settings of different climates in four, permanent exhibits: Palm House, Tropical House, Desert House, and Rainforest.

Lush Retreat *(opposite)*

Brilliantly-patterned coleus and lush ferns are a small sampling of Krohn Conservatory's extensive collection of over 3,500 plant species. Children delight in the annual Summer Butterfly Show when the gardens are filled with fluttering exotic butterflies.

Eden Park

Dense trees cover the hillside of a small section of
Eden Park. Filled with more attractions than any
other city park, the park is busy all year long with
walkers, joggers, skaters, and cyclists, as well as
events at the city's nationally acclaimed art museum
and botanical conservatory.

Keeping Time *(top)*

This beautiful botanical clock, located at Krohn Conservatory, is an actual, working timepiece with flowers that decorate its face. The clock reflects an ancient Greek and Roman tradition that used the opening and closing of different flowers' petals to mark the exact time of day.

Krohn Conservatory *(bottom)*

Among the pathways of Krohn Conservatory is a unique desert experience that incorporates plants and wildlife usually found in far more arid regions. One of four climates featured at this Eden Park conservatory, a variety of rich cacti and succulents bring an otherwise solitary location to life.

Eden Park Gazebo

Built in 1904, the historic, springhouse gazebo at
Eden Park replaced a straw springhouse. For many
years, the natural spring was thought to have pow-
erful, medicinal qualities. The picturesque gazebo
overlooks the reservoir and provides a welcome,
shady respite for cooling off on a hot, summer day.

Tropical Rainforest *(top and bottom)*

The rainforest section of the Krohn Conservatory has an abundance of rich and varied plant life found in lush rainforest regions. The setting, complete with natural waterfall, is housed in a glass-domed environment which is a breeding ground for the most varied plants and animals on Earth.

45

Sawyer Point Historical Markers

The once-run-down waterfront is now one of Cincinnati's newest and most entertaining downtown parks. Created to celebrate the city's bicentennial, Sawyer Point's historic walkway is lined with markers that highlight the area's heritage. The landscaping and park buildings are uniquely designed to reflect the undulating curves of the Ohio River. Cincinnatians find plenty of reasons to come to this riverfront park: summer concerts, playgrounds, picnic areas, and beautiful panoramic views of the river and city.

Cincinnatus Statue at Sawyer Point

When Cincinnati was founded in 1788, it was named Losantville. The name was changed two years later by Arthur St. Clair, governor of the Northwest Territory. St. Clair belonged to the Society of the Cincinnati, an organization that honored George Washington and his sometime comparison, Cincinnatus—Roman general and dictator from the 5th century BC. Though they were separated in time by thousands of years, both men were considered models of Roman virtue and simplicity. Both served their countries, led their armies to victory, and then quietly retired to their farms.

Lucius Quinctus Pigasus

Cincinnati was the long-time center of the Mid-west's successful pork-processing industry. That "can-do" attitude, reflected by the flying-pig theme, is evident all over town in similar statuary. *Lucius Quinctus Pigasus* resides in Sawyer Point Park and is the whimsy of artist Eric Reed Greiner.

Sawyer Point (*above*)

During the summer months, Sawyer Point is busy with concerts and festivals. The wide promenade is often bustling with people enticed by the natural beauty of the area. Scenic lookout areas along the way provide places to pause and enjoy the sweeping, panoramic river views.

The City of Seven Hills (*pages 50–51*)

Before settlers arrived from the East in the late 18th century, Cincinnati was an operative river crossing for local Native-American tribes. Surrounded by more hills than any other city in Ohio, Cincinnati was soon nicknamed the City of Seven Hills: Mount Adams, Walnut Hills, Mount Auburn, Vine Street Hill, Fairmont, Mount Harrison and College Hill. Since its establishment, modern-day Cincinnati has grown to encompass more than those original hills.

Daniel Carter Beard Bridge *(top and bottom)*

Bridges can be both engineering marvels and monumental works of art. The artistic interpretation of Cincinnati's Beard Bridge is appreciated in this detailed view of its dramatic symmetry and graceful lines. Its local namesake is remembered as one of the founders of the Boy Scouts of America.

Canticle *(opposite)*

Russian-born Alexander Liberman created this joyous sculpture as a "hymn of praise soaring in space to elevate the spirit of the spectator." The bold steel sculpture is located on the plaza of Adams Landing, a downtown condominium complex with views of Friendship Park, the river, and nearby hills.

Rubber Duck Regatta *(top and bottom)*

Every Labor Day weekend, more than 70,000 rubber ducks take over the Ohio River during the Rubber Duck Regatta, a famous Cincinnati tradition. Spectators adopt a duck for five dollars and the chance to win a car. All proceeds go to the Freestore Food Bank.

National Steamboat Monument *(opposite)*

This interactive sculpture at the Steamboat Hall of Fame gives spectators more than a passive art experience. It features the original paddlewheel of the riverboat *American Queen* and two dozen smokestacks with sensors that set off whistling and hissing steam jets when approached.

Cincinnati Museum Center *(pages 56–57)*

Swirls of yellow, orange, and gold, accentuated by bands of silver, rise ten stories high in the stunning rotunda of the Cincinnati Museum Center. It houses the Cincinnati History Museum, Museum of Natural History and Science, and Duke Energy Children's Museum and OMNIMAX Theater.

SCRIPPS HOWARD
NEWSREEL THEATER

CINERGY
CHILDREN'S MUSEUM

History in Mosaics

The rotunda of the Cincinnati Museum Center is decorated with Union Terminal's original mosaic murals—the magnificent work of German-born artist Winold Reiss. The 1930s murals detail the history of America, the transportation industry, and the growth and development of Cincinnati. Fore-ground figures are twelve feet tall and depict Americans at work through the centuries, from Native-Americans, to frontier settlers, to modern-day laborers. The golden era of railroads declined after the 1940s, but in 1990, Union Terminal was rescued, and is now the Cincinnati Museum Center.

The History of America

These impressive mosaic murals have three distinctive styles and levels. The workers in the foreground are the most prominent. Behind them, the middle ground illustrates the history of transportation, from horses and oxen-drawn covered wagons, to railroads, steamships, and airplanes. The background of the murals becomes more abstract, changing from rural fields to bustling cities. Originally, artist Winold Reiss created fourteen murals for Union Terminal's concourse area. They can be seen at Cincinnati/Northern Kentucky International Airport.

Aronoff Center For The Arts

Designed by internationally-renowned architect Cesar Pelli, the Aronoff Center for the Arts features three performance spaces and the Weston Art Gallery. Proctor and Gamble Hall is a spacious 2719-seat venue for major performances. The Jarson-Kaplan Theater, a 437-seat venue, creates an intimate, live theater experience. The Fifth Third Theater is a 150-seat studio theater, ideal for theater, dinners, dances, and events. With this variety of performance spaces, the center stays busy with diverse events that draw Greater Cincinnatians to the downtown area.

STANLEY J. ARONOFF CENTER FOR THE ARTS

Architectural Update *(top and bottom)*

Walls of glass flood the lobbies, hallways, and stair-cases of the Aronoff Center with soft natural light. A master of public building design, Cesar Pelli's use of glass and brick creates a modern structure that enhances and blends with older, downtown archi-tecture. Elegant, geometric design details such as stripes, grids, and checkerboards, connect the building's elements inside and out. Many riveting performances of the Cincinnati Ballet are held here in the Proctor and Gamble Hall and the Jarson-Kaplan Theater.

Contemporary Arts Center (*opposite*)

Noted architect Zaha Hadid created the avant-garde design of the Contemporary Arts Center. The offset lines, angular features, color, and mix of material forms make even staircases reflect the structural art that is inherent in the building's theme. The center features bold exhibits of new, contemporary artists.

Sculpture in Motion (*above*)

Late sculptor George Rickey was one of the first to introduce "moving" sculpture. Rickey's 1979 piece, *Two Rectangles Vertical Gyratory II Variation IV* is an important example of kinetic sculpture. Two large paddles move at random in a perpetual dance atop a tall shaft, located outside of the PNC Center.

Shillito's Clock *(above)*

"Meet me under the clock at McAlpin's." For ninety-eight years, people have rendezvoused under the elegant Shillito's Clock. Recently, the vintage timepiece moved to a new location in front of the old Chester Park train station at the Heritage Village Museum, a 19th-century historic village.

Starbursts *(opposite)*

Cincinnati's heralded Labor Day festivities begin long before dark at Sawyer Point Park. By mid-afternoon, crowds begin to gather for games, food, and live concerts, all which lead up to the spectacular evening fireworks display that explodes over the Ohio River.

Holy Cross Immaculata Church

During a severe 19th-century storm at sea, Archbishop John Patrick Purcell promised God that, if he survived, he would build a church on the highest point in Cincinnati. The historic Roman Catholic Church, built in 1859, sits on the hilltop of the Mt. Adams community, fulfilling his commitment.

Hyde Park Square (top)

Residents of this upscale area of stately homes, estates, apartments, and businesses congregate at "The Square." It's the neighborhood gathering place, complete with a lovely fountain. The Hyde Park Square Art Show is the largest one-day art show in the city.

Historic Mt. Adams Neighborhood (bottom)

Located north of downtown, the historic Mt. Adams neighborhood is nestled on the highest hill in Cincinnati, and has panoramic river and city views. In this charming, historic neighborhood, many of the city's best shops, cafés, and restaurants are tucked between houses on residential streets.

Proctor and Gamble over Mt. Adams *(above)*

The steep-pitched roofs of colorful houses on the edge of the hilltop neighborhood of Mt. Adams are overshadowed by the massive towers of the Proctor and Gamble Headquarters. Convenient to downtown, the Mt. Adams area is known for its charm and trendy, neighborhood clubs and bars.

Walnut Street *(opposite)*

Walnut Street is a fine example of a downtown revitalization success story. Sparked by the opening of the Stanley J. Aronoff Center for Arts, the revitalization has resulted in a heightened area interest and economic draw to adjacent shops, hotels, restaurants, and clubs.

The Book Fountain

The Amelia Valerio Weinberg Memorial Fountain is the centerpiece of the plaza at the Main Library. Nicknamed "the book fountain," this delightful fountain, by sculptor Michael Frasca, symbolizes the free flow of ideas and information through the printed word. The books are made of ceramic tile.

Music Hall Over-the-Rhine

Cincinnati's elegant Music Hall overlooks the enduring Over-the-Rhine neighborhood that was originally settled by German immigrants. The 1878 structure is a spectacular example of High Victorian Gothic Revival architecture. Inside, a mural depicts artists and events in the Music Hall's history.

Cincinnati Fire Museum

Each year, over 25,000 people visit the Cincinnati
Fire Museum. More than half are school children
who get to slide down the pole, run the sirens, and
sit behind the wheel of a fire truck.

Fire-fighting Innovations

Listed in the National Register of Historic Places, this 1907 firehouse is home to the Cincinnati Fire Museum, and honors the 200-year history of the city's fire department. Artifacts include "the pumper"—the first mechanism to successfully pump water from the fire truck directly onto the fire.

William Howard Taft National Historic Site

Born and raised in this 19th-century house on Auburn Avenue, William Howard Taft would become the 27th president of the United States. Taft was the only president to also hold the office of Chief Justice of the United States, which presides over the Supreme Court.

Inside the Taft Family Home (*top and bottom*)

Several rooms in President Taft's boyhood home have been restored, allowing museum-goers to experience the authentic environment in which he was raised. It is easy to imagine guests conversing in the Victorian parlor (*top*), or studying legal journals in the library (*bottom*). Exhibits on the second floor highlight Taft's life and career, and include an animatronic figure of Taft's son, Charlie, relating stories about family members. Members of the Ladies Living History Society of Greater Cincinnati provide tours and model garments that Mrs. Taft would have worn from 1850 to 1870.

Taft Museum of Art

Located in the historic Baum-Longworth-Taft House, the museum features European masters, 19th-century American art, antique furnishings, and decorative arts. The house is one of the oldest wooden structures in the city—a striking example of American-Palladian architecture.

Harriet Beecher Stowe House

In 1850, when Harriet Beecher Stowe wrote *Uncle Tom's Cabin*, a fictional story that dared to challenge the inhumanity of slavery, she unleashed the transforming power of the written word. Her name would become a household word and her story would help to create a public outcry for change.

It is ironic that Stowe, as a 19th-century woman, was forbidden by law to vote, or to speak at a public meeting, and was even denied legal rights. Stowe lived in this house, which is now a public historical and cultural site where visitors learn about the Stowe family's contributions to America.

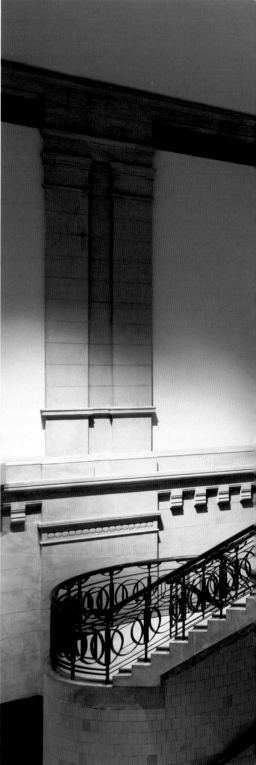

Cincinnati Art Museum

The Cincinnati Art Museum's highly-acclaimed collection travels world-wide, showcasing the history of art through the ages. In 2003, the prestigious museum opened the Cincinnati Wing, the first permanent display of a city's local art history in the nation.

The Art Place of The West

In the late 19th century, the idea for an art museum in Cincinnati took root quickly, as generous citizens made major donations to the venture. The stately art museum opened in scenic Eden Park in 1886 and drew international praise as "The Art Palace of the West." Today, the world-class museum showcases an encyclopedic collection of over 60,000 works of art spanning six-thousand years. During the renovations to Fountain Square in 2006, part of the Tyler Davidson Fountain, *The Genius of Water*, by German artist, August von Kreling, was on temporary display.

Cincinnati Museum Center

The old clock from Union Station's original newspaper stand adorns the entrance to the Cincinnati Museum Center. A modernized, beaux-arts, architectural treasure, the former train station, is now home to the spacious Cincinnati History Museum, one of the largest, urban, history museums in the country; the Museum of Natural History and Science, where you can "Buy a Bone" and help rebuild a dinosaur; the Duke Energy Children's Museum, one of the "Top 25" children's museums in the world; and OMNIMAX Theater, a mega-movie experience on a five-story movie screen.

The Freedom Center (top and bottom)

Students get a history lesson at the National Underground Railroad Freedom Center. The center opened in 2004 in the exact location on the northern bank of the Ohio River where many slaves grasped their first taste of freedom. It chronicles the Underground Railroad, a network of anti-slavery advocates who risked their lives to secretly move runaway slaves from one safe house to another until they reached the freedom of the north—a journey that often covered hundreds of miles. The center is the first facility dedicated to the quest of the enslaved to become free.

Home of the Cincinnati Bengals *(top)*

Paul Brown Stadium is home to the NFL's Cincinnati Bengals. Opened in 2000, the new stadium provides great views of downtown and the Ohio River that fans enjoy pre-game or at half-time. This was the first stadium to be voted one of America's 150 favorite buildings in a Harris Interactive Survey.

Crosley Terrace *(bottom and opposite)*

The rich history of America's first professional baseball club is evident as fans enter the stadium through Crosley Terrace, a nostalgic reminder of Crosley Field, the Cincinnati Reds previous home. The entranceway is dominated by life-size, bronze sculptures of former Reds greats.

Riverside Baseball *(pages 84–85)*

The new Great American Ballpark seats 42,000 fans. It is designed to honor the great riverboat heritage of Cincinnati, with two steamboat smokestacks behind right center field that light up and launch smoke and fireworks to celebrate a home run or to simply encourage the local team.

Cincinnati Reds Hall of Fame

The Hall of Fame for America's first professional baseball team opened in 2003. The facility honors the history of the team, dating from 1869, with multimedia exhibits, photographs, and memorabilia. In the center of the "Glory Days" gallery, individual showcases display the team's three World Series Championship trophies—1975, 1976, and 1990. By 2006, the Reds Hall of Fame had inducted seventy-one top performers, including club players, managers, and executives.

Glory Days Gallery

The Reds Hall of Fame "Glory Days" gallery captures the final play of the 1972 National League Pennant game. Life-size figures of Rose, Griffey, Morgan, Foster, Bench, Perez, Concepcion, and Geronimo celebrate the moment while their announcer, Al Michaels, calls the play. The gallery also commemorates four championship seasons between 1919 and 1990 with photos, artifacts, and players' taped interviews from each era. Now in their new stadium, the Cincinnati Reds begin yet another era of exciting and memorable seasons.

Cincinnati Zoo and Botanical Garden

The Cincinnati Zoo includes an award-winning botanical garden experience with over three-thousand plant varieties from around the world. The zoo and botanical garden's outstanding collection demonstrates how specific plants relate to individual animal species, and how that relation-ship changes from region to region. Outside of the natural settings of the exhibits, the facility includes outstanding herbage and garden displays in a scenic, park setting for the education and enjoyment of all visitors.

Riding a Rhino

The nation's second oldest zoo dates back to 1875 and is a National Historic Landmark. It houses over five-hundred animal species. This top-ranked zoo is an internationally-recognized leader in education and conservation efforts that focus on saving endangered species around the world. Attendees of the zoo's newly-renovated Sumatran rhino exhibit will not only see this great animal up close, but will learn about the breakthroughs in research that are helping to save the world's most endangered rhino species.

Oktoberfest on Purple People Bridge

Energetic musicians climb to the top of the Purple
People Bridge during Cincinnati's world-famous
Oktoberfest. The festival began as a block party
near Fountain Square in 1976 to celebrate the city's
rich German heritage, and has grown into the
largest Oktoberfest event in North America.

Oktoberfest Offerings *(top and bottom)*

Over 500,000 people travel from near and far to attend Oktoberfest, Cincinnati's biggest party, where everything German is done on a grand scale. Crowds consume 80,000 bratwursts, 24,000 potato pancakes, and more German beer than most are willing to measure. Oktoberfest in Cincinnati holds the *Guinness Book* world record for the largest group of people dancing the popular German "Chicken Dance." The event's dance leaders have included celebrities such as trumpeter Al Hirt, Tony Orlando, and Weird Al Yankovic.

Historic Clock Tower

A familiar, four-sided clock tower rises high above the historic Campbell County Courthouse, show-casing the fine details of the building's Late Victorian, Classical Revival architectural style. Located within the Greater Cincinnati area, the courthouse serves a county-wide population of over 88,000 residents. This is the only county in Kentucky that has two courthouses. The first was built in Alexandria.

Campbell County Courthouse

The official Campbell County seat of government was moved to Newport, Kentucky in 1797. The historic courthouse opened for business in 1884. The Victorian brick building, with its marble floors and stained-glass window, was placed on the National Register of Historic Places in 1988.

Riverwalk, Newport on The Levee (*opposite*)

Newport's historic Riverwalk at Newport on the Levee features views of the beautiful Ohio River and the sparkling skyline of Cincinnati. This trendy district offers shopping, entertainment, video game amusements, art galleries, and the Newport Aquarium.

World Peace Bell (*above*)

Newport, Kentucky hosts the largest, free-swinging bell in the world: the Millennium Monument. A symbol of freedom and peace, the thirty-three-ton bell was designed and cast by the Verdin Company in Cincinnati, the largest supplier of bells, carillons, and clocks in the world.

Mitchell's Fish Market

Mitchell's is such a popular restaurant in Greater
Cincinnati that it received *Cincinnati Magazine's*
Reader's Choice Award. The remarkable menu fea-
tures fresh seafood from the frigid waters of the
Bering Strait, to the deep waters off the coast of
Chile, all served in an upscale, nautical setting.

Newport Aquarium

Newport Aquarium sports a nautical motif with soaring masts that rise above the roofline. On the Kentucky side of the Ohio River, the aquarium features seventy exhibits of amazing sea life from around the world. Clear, acrylic tunnels transport visitors through the ocean, surrounded by teeming sea life, just inches away. Sharks participate in a feeding frenzy at dinner time, and youngsters delight at the antics of the penguins. Older children can pack their overnight bags for occasional "Sleep with the Sharks" slumber parties.

Wonders of The Deep

The excitement of the Newport Aquarium begins
with a big splash at the front door. Inside, you are
surrounded by sea creatures. A massive whale
comes up for air and fills the room with his power.
Giant seahorses and other strange and wonderful
creatures are suspended in mid-air.

Gallons of Fun

The white, sandy bottom of the ocean floor is seen through a bubble window at the Newport Aquarium. In this ethereal and soundless world, big sharks rule the domain and blanket the view with their massive shapes, while groups of smaller fish dart past the opening.

Circling Sharks

In the Newport Aquarium, 200-foot-long, acrylic
tunnels provide an incredible, yet safe, vantage
point for visitors as they walk within inches of
intimidating killer sharks—some at least ten-feet-
long.

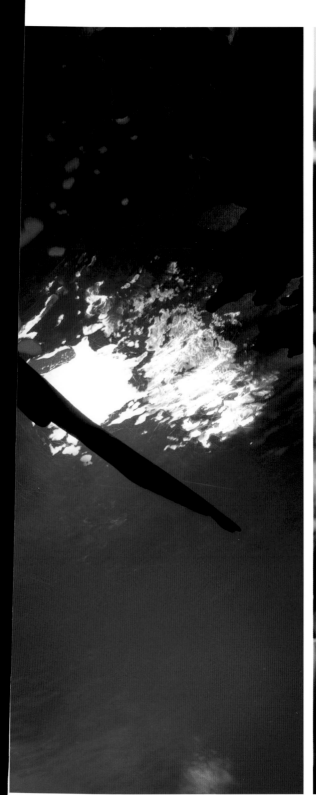

Live Music on the Levee

A young boy strums along with the musicians at a summer concert at Newport on the Levee. This popular tourist spot comes alive during the summer with live concerts and festivals. During the colder months, the beat goes on every day at Jefferson Hall with local and regional bands.

Labor Day Riverfest (top)

Crowds on the Newport, Kentucky riverbank gather at noon on Labor Day weekend in anticipation of the fantastic fireworks display held later that night along the river. On the Cincinnati side, spectators line the riverfront between the Public Landing and Sawyer Point for an equally-spectacular view.

Annual Powerboat Races (bottom)

Top powerboat racers across the country are in the driver's seat of these sleek machines at Cincinnati's world-class ChampBoat Grand Prix. The race starts in Newport on the Levee, Kentucky, and runs one-and-one-half miles down the Ohio River. This is North America's premier powerboat racing series.

Greater Cincinnati ChampBoat Grand Prix

High-tech, aerodynamic speedboats race to the finish at the Champboat Grand Prix. Top boat-racing teams from across the country come to participate in this exciting powerboat-racing series. Cincinnati is one of twelve cities between Connecticut and Colorado that host this prestigious event.

James Bradley Statue, Covington, Kentucky *(above)*

This pensive statue recognizes the accomplishments of former slave, James Bradley. At the age of eighteen, Bradley managed an Arkansas plantation and, five years later, was able to buy his freedom. He was the only ex-slave to participate in the famous Lane Seminary Debates on Slavery and Abolitionism.

Daniel Carter Beard *(opposite)*

One of the founders of the Boy Scouts of America, Daniel Carter Beard is honored in this bronze statue by noted sculptor Kenneth Bradford. It is located near Beard's boyhood home in Covington, Kentucky. Beard was also a social reformer, author, and artist who illustrated books for Mark Twain.

Cathedral Basilica of the Assumption *(opposite)*

The magnificent Gothic-style cathedral in Coving-ton, Kentucky, is one of only thirty-five minor basil-icas in the United States; all major basilicas are in Rome. The cathedral's spectacular windows include the world's largest stained-glass window installed in a church, measuring 67 by 24 feet in length.

Wright Cycle Company *(top)*

Before the Wright brothers traveled to a North Carolina beach to test their flying machines on steady ocean breezes, they were inquisitive chil-dren, growing up in Dayton, Ohio. It was here, in the back room of their bicycle shop, that they first tested aerodynamic principles with bicycle parts.

Initially they built gliders, then, three years later, they arrived at Kitty Hawk, North Carolina with their daring flying innovation—a contribution that would pave the way for modern transportation.

Angels over Dayton

The amazing Blue Angels headline the Dayton Air Show. They are the ultimate showmanship team of high-flying precision. The air show also features world-class aerobatic champions coaxing their planes to perform thrilling loops, dives, and 180-degree fly-bys.

National Museum of The United States Air Force

Two-hundred years of miltary aircraft history are documented in the museum's complex of hangars at Wright Patterson Air Force Base in Vandalia, Ohio, located approximately fifty miles north of Cincinnati. Included is the B-29 bomber that was instrumental in World War II's Pacific outcome.

Amidst the sleek aircraft in the Cold War gallery, the Stealth Bomber impressively demonstrates the power of modern technology.

Delta Formation

The Blue Angels of the United States Navy exhibit
their renowned six-jet Delta Formation in F/A-18
Hornets at the Dayton Air Show and at thirty-four
other air shows throughout the year. The squadron
was named after the "Blue Angel Nightclub" in
New York during its first season in 1946.

F/A-18 Hornet (*top*)

The resilient F/A-18 Hornet was the first aircraft to have carbon fiber wings, and the first tactical jet fighter to use digital, fly-by-wire flight controls. After 1986, it was the hands-down favorite for the United States Navy's Blue Angels, who traded in their A-4 Skyhawks for the Hornets.

Dayton Air Show (*bottom*)

Because of their obvious differences, these two aircraft fly together only for a mere second. The two were designed fifty years apart. The 1940's era P-38 Lightning bomber can't reach 300 mph. The F-16 Fighting Falcon slows to 400 mph. They perform over the Wright Brothers' hometown.

Ferocious Roller Coasters

From the terrifying king of all roller coasters, "Beast," to the "Rugrats Runaway Reptar," Kings Island has a crowd-pleasing variety of thrilling rides over twisty tracks, or in this case, suspended under the tracks, with lovable characters from the *Rugrats* cartoon as your companions.

Carousel Smiles

For youngsters, a slow and gentle ride on a zebra or horse is a relaxing pause between wilder rides at King's Island, such as the fast-paced "Shake, Rattle & Roll" ride, or the "Fairly Odd Coaster"—perfect for those who are not quite ready for the more-challenging amusements.

Son-of-Beast

"Son of Beast" is the tallest and fastest wooden roller coaster in the world. Its fellow coaster, "Beast," is the longest wooden coaster. These are just two of over forty thrill-rides at this top-ranked amusement park, just twenty-four miles north of Cincinnati.

Ohio Renaissance Festival *(above and right)*

Each weekend for seven weeks in the fall, costumed performers live the life-medieval in a recreated English village in Harveysburg, Ohio. Jousting tournaments, storytellers, strolling musicians, singers, dancers, and regular village folk provide a taste of medieval times gone by.

Championship Match (pages 118–119)

Andy Roddick (USA) and Juan Ferrero (Spain) compete in the 2006 Western and Southern Financial ATP Masters at the Lindner Family Tennis Center in Mason, Ohio. It is the only venue outside of the Grand Slams that has more than two permanent stadiums.

AVP Crocs, Mason (above)

Though not a sea-side city, Cincinnati has become a top, professional beach volleyball destination. Players Paige Davis and Kerri Walsh face each other at the net in the 2006 AVP Crocs Cincinnati Open. The major volleyball event is broadcast nationally.

Beach Volleyball

Enthusiastic fans crowd the stands during the season-ending, world-class AVP Tour championship. The event signed an historic, long-term deal with Cincinnati to host the championship through 2011.

Paddling the River

The Whitewater River and the Lower Little Miami River provide paddling challenges with pristine beauty. The Lower Little Miami is Ohio's first designated "Wild and Scenic River." The river's rapids, rolling banks, and natural vegetation provide the ultimate kayaking experience.

Tubing on East Fork Lake

Two youngsters hold on tight as their tube flies across the water, pulled by a powerboat's tow rope. The rivers and lakes around Cincinnati give boating enthusiasts plenty of space to enjoy their favorite water sport, whether it's high-speed waterskiing, rafting, or slower-paced canoeing or kayaking.

Turfway Park

Colorful jockeys greet visitors at Turfway Park in Florence, Kentucky. Turfway's predecessor, Latonia Race Course, opened in 1883. In 1986, the track was renamed "Turfway Park." It is located about seventy-five miles from Churchill Downs in Louisville, home to the prestigious Kentucky Derby.

Horse Power *(above)*

Turfway Park provides live thoroughbred racing action during fall, winter, and early spring, as well as large-screen simulcasts of major races across the country. Turfway was the first horse-racing track in North America to use a hybrid vinyl track that is safer for horses and riders.

The Sport of Kings *(pages 126–127)*

Thoroughbred hooves pound the track as spectators watch a weekday race at Turfway Park. In 1994, the park introduced a major racing event, the Kentucky Cup Day of Champions, which features five stakes races that precede the Breeders' Cup championship.